HAWT

C000111333

TONY WILLIAMS

Hawthorn City

SALT

CROMER

PUBLISHED BY SALT PUBLISHING 2019

2 4 6 8 10 9 7 5 3 1

Copyright © Tony Williams 2019

Tony Williams has asserted his right under the Copyright, Designs and Patents Act 1988 to be identified as the author of this work.

This book is sold subject to the condition that it shall not, by way of trade or otherwise, be lent, resold, hired out, or otherwise circulated without the publisher's prior consent in any form of binding or cover other than that in which it is published and without a similar condition including this condition being imposed on the subsequent publisher.

First published in Great Britain in 2019 by
Salt Publishing Ltd
12 Norwich Road, Cromer, Norfolk NR27 0AX United Kingdom

www.saltpublishing.com

Salt Publishing Limited Reg. No. 5293401

A CIP catalogue record for this book is available from the British Library

ISBN 978 1 78463 212 0 (Paperback edition)

Typeset in Sabon by Salt Publishing

Printed and bound in Great Britain by Clays Ltd, Elcograf S.p.A

To Fred

Contents

HAWTHORN CITY

Cheviotica

up the moor
on me tod
a boiled egg
& sod the lot

Hawthorn City

In May I think another
city opens out, a city
built of air and hawthorn.
Its rathaus is a stile
and daylight leaping
over the midnight
cattle of midsummer.

(Articulated lorries
cross the bridge
I'm walking with the dog
this winter morning.)
On those branching streets
slow down
the walls of stony time
that house us in.

The hawthorn city speaks
behind the dozing backs of cows
a promise and command:
Unmake the law
(I'm on the bus), *let
each day shimmer
as both yesterday
and the long tomorrow.
And let each hour
be its own, forever.*

A city's nothing but its people.
A hedge is nothing but
its blossom, every blossom
a window on a room
where insects spin
around a dusty yucca.
I'm sitting in the room,
and you are too (perhaps
you're working in an office)

while soft as ash or
midnight fog the whisper
of that future chokes
down grey arterials,
and as the herd departs, the city
passes with its light
and season, leaving
a fragrant archive in the air.

I will always be its citizen.

Walk I

To leap the gate
    and bless the hinge
that turns aside
    where I impinge

to palm the egg
    and wring the throat
and douse my hair
    with creosote

to hide my name
    inside a cough
and charm the lamb
    I'd carry off

to make a fire
    in my hat
to guard the silence
    of my path

Winter, 1982

Lighting the fire on a
winter's morning
good news that we'll be
in all day

maybe you'll climb inside
the radio and maybe
the snow will start to fall
outside the glass and lunch

will stretch over many decades
the teapot's hot breast
and the fire's crackle
the smell of soot and

the carpet's patterned dust
so hard to read the
inky branches
in the field all this

in the grate and your fingers
quick with dry ash
like indoor snow your knees
on the hard hearth

how lonely you must have been
just you and the youngest
another day of cold
and nothing we spun through

as different stars

My Mother Working

She's not good company. She ignores
all but the problem of the one mask
and how to show what it shows
of the living it hides inside itself –
a matter of subtraction, knocking off
what flesh she had slapped on
to a bodged armature of wood
and chicken wire. How handfuls
torn from a bucket fatten
the blunt skull and begin to flatter
the words *temple*, *nose*, *brow*
into being. You watch her
smudge with her thumb a contour
away as she would a smut
by her child's eye, or lick her thumb
to turn the page of a newspaper
or conjure at a moment of need
the jack of diamonds and play it.

It is a tide of clay
going on and coming off, the hands
wiped on the smock and the golem
anointed with water to keep it quick.
She steps backwards and looks
at the grave-bust in its wreath
of Polaroids and sketches, or stares
accusingly at the sitter.

You watch her pare clay likeness
to unlikeness to likeness with tools

like a torturer's. You watch her
gouge at nostril and ear, then smooth
to airlessness the deaf particulate
paste in irritation. She keeps
destroying; the thing is made
not by accumulation but the learned
finesse of going over moves
a thousand times and knowing
when to end it. Some days she'll stop,
tie on the shroud of plastic sheeting,
and leave for a glass of wine;
the problem will throb all night
in her dumb fingers. Every morning
she begins again, hopeless and confident.

What she is trying to achieve
is simple, she says. She says
it is not a matter, how could it,
of making the head real
in every detail, at all angles. A fool
if you think the breath will come
when the head turns and the mouth
opens to thank her. What the clay
cannot do cannot
be made to happen. It is a matter
of giving it life: in the tides of art, of seeing
one glance one profile one shadow

when the sum of clay and the long
untotalled columns of a person

coincide for a second, and a whiff
or a knack or a way or a phrase
of that person's cadence opens
just in that aspect, it has a look of them,
and you step away, she says,
from the shape of your own limits
as work and these kilos of clay make them.

A Mask of Wyn Sanders

1

Why does she sit there
this dead woman
defiantly in the lavender?

Her blank eyes watch
the bees wobble.
Her set frown

at nothing gathers
moss and shrivels
what alights there.

Large whites fly
the flags of themselves
in front of her.

2

Garden to leaven the grave,
grave to tell the garden why.
Face a concrete shadow

to enjoy the season's passage
and whisper through wild
strawberries' décolletage:

You too will go where I have gone.
I stayed to show the way
because my friend conjured.

3

Now that my friends
are dying one by one
I see what it is

my mother has been doing
all her life
she has made.

She shares it with the dead.
By looking she confirmed
she saw. By making

she made the garden
unalone, the garden
of her friends herself

around the absence of
her own face when
that stone stops looking.

Walk II

The vagrant snoring
    under maps
the teeth that bite
    the local lips

the vagrant eye
    that wants to see
all ditches'
    immortality

the vagrant light
    that infiltrates
by broken fence
    the large estates

the vagrant feet
    that scuff and go
away from every
    way you know

The Heights of Abraham and the Heights of Jacob

The house was like a chimney giving vent
to what it was that burned inside the hill.
Our tongues were kippered
in that shed of fumes. It was
a house of glass that made
exhibits of the rooks against
far velvet woodlands
with their bones exposed.

Its stone shivered and shrugged
our decades from it and remained.

Its door is always open and I rise
as demon up its stairwell, rattling boards
to scare the me within. I am
the haunting of my own bewilderment.

It was myself I shared that silence with,
the candidate and no less the flame
that waits to test his mettle
in the dining room. The chair legs
make an olive grove or cage
for keeping till the sacrificial hour.

To hell with world, your world is hell
and let your planet burn. It's just for me
this house is all there is and living here.
Inside the ossuary of love I know
the graveyard teased the beetle for a while.

It was the valley and the darkling birds
looked on some pupae which the house displayed.

Thanksgiving for a Chest Infection

I lie dizzy under
the glass of illness
like a cucumber.
Pills and water, pinching
out the tissue flowers –
how this garden grows me.

If you cut me open
you would bare
the wet seeds that make
my lungs crackle.
Meanwhile a mouse
is running round the bed's
edges nibbling
at stray shoots and thoughts
and that is part of
the bargain of a body foxed
in its fruiting.

Here pinned a pale
moth I listen
to a bird's insistence
invisible outside
the open window.
Here still never
moving I listen
to an under hum
of air that world is
only when you step
away and seal the space

between you with the glass
of slow reactions.

Me and something only
mine and no one else's
share this sweat and stillness,
a conversation whispered
in shallow breaths, a wedding
night stretching over bright
weekdays and closed
in a jeweller's case
of sweet infected air –
my illness, my gift
that has given glass
bulkheads to make this voyage
for a time my own
and only mine again
shared with my body
remembering the pleasure
of sleeping and thinking how
in an hour I'll manage
and share it with the mouse
a slice of toast and honey.

What Mam Threw on the Fire

The carcass of a chicken,
a brace of mouldy boots,
everything that's broken,
anything that suits,

a pair of rabbit's britches,
the scrapings of the sauce,
all the window latches,
all the open doors,

heaped potato peelings
then the naked spuds –
spectres of the coals –
and gravy by the jug,

a box, a bruise, a feather,
dustpans full of dust,
time to wonder whether
what she burns is what she must.

Can she burn the river?
Should she burn the woods?
When she burns such treasures
do they burn for good?

How Tom Fell Down High Tor

A dark he's seen so often now
to leave the pubshut ribboned road
and rise by ivy slopes beside
the fractured yellow cliff to take
the drunken fathomable path
the tails of his coat like scree
      my brother fell a satellite
      by gravel stars a calcite stream
      the brook of time that broke apart
      the ropes that hold a feeling there
      to flay his back and lurch his heart
      a loss of breath he gambled by
and in the fall a wince of air
before his body kisses pain
to nearly close the gorge of death
synaptic as a keenish glance
not taken up but keep his feet
and leave one star at the cliff's foot
      and walking home on every night
      to step again on the loose stones
      in a grazed river meet himself
      as stone air still imagines him
      one night in monument
      the tipsy, incomplete surprise

The Flower Time

When I stagger back
with a broken jaw
gasping out for water
burned by the law

I'll find, I know, the village
shorn of other moments
showering the petals
of the flower time

over all else
and the stone I've travelled.
Blossom will be shadow.
Blossom will be light.

Here will be no centre
but a place to rest
on a longer journey,
her only voicing

the echo that I bring
and a little hill
standing by the river,
the train and the road

woven in the valley
at the juncture of my living
by the breath of her breathing,
the fabric of love.

A Song for Masson Hill

I sing for the hill
a monolith that leans
away to leave
its dark galena heart
a closed proscenium
where a figure stands
on the skyline of a tale.

There the copper ferns
dissolve in rain to run
by a slender clough
towards the secret cliff
that has the house's back
and a thin fire tends
to smoke its melody.

There cattle deny
the right of way and rain
fills the stile to wash
the daytime clean of talk.
I sing how the hill's
music is the ground
of every walk. I sing

landscape like a bed
imprinted with her form
the lonely mother or
the smiling girl who went
through pastured slopes

where grubby fungi keep
their mild toxins close.

The song is a lane
whose camber tilts the boot
towards the line that makes
a charm or hex around
an almond of rock
where the hillside hums:

Inside this space
it can't get me
except in dreams

Only in dreams
can I get
inside this space

Helgafell

There is a quarry in my heart. The lovely lanes
divide. One humps from Upperwood to Uppertown
by Ember Lane, and Ember Farm (my family's farm,
which has not been our farm for fifty years).
At Bonsall's market cross, the clot of stone
sends tassels out towards the Barley Mow, the moor,
and down towards the valley's narrow chute
that lands with laughing splashes at the pond
at Scarthin. There's a bookshop here,
so it's safe to leave us,
while we retrace and take the other fork
down by the Wapping and the last few houses,
Christine's and the Warnes' and this one on the left
which had an empty pond and concrete turtle,
a totem of the presence on the hill
whose cloak of bramble, altar which we raided,
prevented every ingress. Through the woods –
to skirt with steps like murmurs St John's Chapel,
Shining Cliff, the Heights of Jacob,
and there, below, the red mill and its chimney
and the path down into Scarthin where the swans
are waiting by the bookshop, and we find
ourselves perusing Local Interest
for a book to help us, but no geology
can name a space from which the stone has gone.

Walk III

A muddy dog
   is passing by
the final house
   away from here
to stand around
   the dog at heel
then slip the lead
   and wonder there
at the wide cliff
   above the woods
the gateless posts
   and footpath sign
the gulls-and-sewage
   whirl of air

a chain and nail
   knocking to
the chirr of cars
   a greasy road
that's heading north
   and out of here
the bridge's lean
   and shaky arc
the legs that thread
   around again

and knit the days
   to loop and cross
the smirking dog
   a satellite

to scare the birds
    and gain the ridge
and lift the hare
    and panting pause
to sit and wait
    at the broad root
the dog's head turned
    away from here

to lose a boot
    in green lanes' guts
more stuck than go
    with collar up
to carve the wind
    a stalled machine
the dropping track
    and collie on
a pick-up's back

and turning off
    towards the town
to drop between
    the shore and sky
going here
    and going back
the breakfast things
    congealing yolk
to welcome home
    the secret twinge
in walkers' strides

        and close the old
unsurveyed path
        that takes its load
outside all law
        and the difficult
ordinary way

Hero at the Cave

Behind the frozen foss
there is a hollow place
a cave beneath the law
sky-wide and full of moss
and wethers' yellow knucks
dispersed as runes
in drifts of fleece and dogs
reporting close pursuit
men's shouts running
round a black filled lung
the flooded church and drowned
community of thought
towards the monster's den
where partisans stack
their rifles and disrobe
the blackened spuds that lie
hiding in the stones

The icy gate is shut
but you will drop a rope
to kill and clear the space
sacred to a time
that spurns turfen huts
as a modern pose
but don't know which you slay
the troll which makes the dark-
ness constant or the band
who keep a fire there
against all governments

And when your blade is wet
you pass through moving glass
strike out away uphill
towards the moor and stare
at curlews' falling calls
the droppings like shot
cached by every stream
where what voices come
scare the plateau flat
the paths that aged rains
and starving hares demand
of sand and peat and in
whose kinks your feet are turned
and snared

Scraped skull of land
store of guns and fire
in the rigid heart
the unrespected wire
of the borderings
lie down and let the marsh-
land seethe your mind to sleep
then wake absolved of all
the rage and gnarling talk
of earth up on the moors
your body speaks
this rash of bursted fruit
where you laid across
the bilberry banks
a shibboleth or taint

which says that you must stay
out beyond the farms

Stalk deep prints
bless the frozen groughs
returning to the stone
dizzy gulf that waits
with water's zealous No
the stalled lurch of what
can't be denied but can
perhaps be stayed
for a single living night
the ice-curtained cave
cranny like a mouth
leaving much unsaid
where nowt could be worse
except the leaving now

Here the losers hide
amongst a monster's bones
and you must choose
to join them or arrest
the ones who won't give up
their tomb of principle
whose sly recess means
We do not consent
foregoing love and hearth
for the sake of love
as you forsake the sky
for this high crystal vault

A Nap after Laxness

To lie down on the cliff
a spotted handkerchief
and fall to daisies' sleep
by a gull-spun slip
and crash through sleeping's sneeze
and by the sky to reach
the bright cloud Claudette

The smocked nurses watch
the snoring faller pass
with teaset eye and beak
a nib dipped to set
the secret rubric out
how things could be
one leaping morning for
the boy and Claudette

The gospel of the drop
which teaches love
from stone's height to stone
memorial beneath
the ice anointing sea
which squeezes sleep
to snuff however good
the dream and by its lurch
wake the waistcoat and
the girl in daylight's breeze
a single tear and voice
that glisters through the calls

of gulls beside the cliff
asking for the gift
of sleep: Claudette, Claudette

The Count

Yaina, taina, eddera, eke
Peddera, seddera, my pal Pete
In the know and in the street
Layter, tayter, bumfitt, speak

Ovvera, covvera, pipsole, dix
Arno, jiggit, brono, stix
Lunka, munka, ittera, quix
One two three four five six

Mumph and hither and lither and stop
Helter, skelter, lucky bone, drop
Pitheran titheran rum tum tot
No and never and nowt and not

Edderax, pedderax, tic a bub, toon
Yainobumfitt, afternoon
After laughter, polish and spit
Fottery, fat as a fat dog's shit

Yertz a comfit, grey grass grew
Under your feet und draust bist du
Dix and yaindix, jaundice, John
has taken off his trousers on

Bilo tenera quincunx drain
Vomitus up in court again
Nihil mortes ex abyss
Nought in total less than this

Gorse

Gorse's knuckles cracking
fire without its flames
there the figure beckons
every child to run

high above the bracken
and by the wall to name
the curlew's eerie whistle
sombre as a game

by the ruined bastle
placid horses stand
waiting for the colic
that kills them in the end

the feeble alcoholic's
left a wash of rum
in his other pocket
thirsting bangs its drum

the tree has lost its blossom
fruit has lost its tang
far from mummy's bosom
every thief must hang

The Devil's Hand

I saw the devil's hand laid on the grass
outstretched to grab the ankles as they pass
of good girls and the drunk and men-at-arms
who chase bad luck before them through the farms
where barley sickens and the people say
our Sarah's visage is a touch more grey
since he who hates us crept into her bed
and for this crime she must be punishèd
and after praying they sit down to eat
what seems to them a board of fruit and meat
her womanhood and humbles furnished out
a kiss goodbye to blush the pitcher's spout
all this being etched upon the palm that lay
dissevered from the law and on the way
from hardship on to something else that night
I hurried onwards to unsee my sight

An Old Funeral

The night that followed the woman's wake
the door was open half a creak
and the babies cried for the new god's sake
and the whispering tawse was smart was quick
as a knife blade used as a candlewick
a mother asleep in a gown of gorse
No not for you in a lover's face

To visit grief is a priest's reward
from a round bone jug his fee is poured
he drinks and drinks and toasts his Lord
from a leathern old three-handled tyg
and shares that brew with a fox and a pig
This is Mr Pennies-on-the-Eyes
This is Mistress Meat
she sugared her tale to make it sweet
No not for you, No not for you

She sold her hand and hid the gold
in her pinny's pouch, she shut up the cold
in a mouth whose teeth were only an old
sow's knuckles she prayed to the wrong god
so now she is dead
and the stream runs black at the ford
and everyone knows what the sexton said

So strangle the dusk that breathes in the lane
and hammer a shoe on a standing stane
so that the devil may ride again
and worry the ewes before they bear

the blind lambs, find the square
of linen that caught your lover's kisses
as her voice whispers
Not for you, No not for you, my love

The Felton Sycamores

Following the Battle of Dunbar, Cromwell's army force-marched 5,000 Scottish prisoners south to England. Most died on the way or after arriving in Durham; the rest were sold into slavery in the Americas.

There grow inside my head
on the Felton Road
three trees: the Starving
and the Sick, and Those
who will survive to go
across England's ocean.

The Scottish soldiers stood
between Dunbar's red stone,
that hard place the Kirk,
an English Devil and
the grey North Sea,
and having lost were taken

on a tramping way
that the world knows well,
a people passing by
with foreign voices
towards a something worse
that human pasts will mourn

but only landscape notice
at the hour of its passing:
how a sapling saw
the march without a morsel

and shedding dead like seeds
so that has thickened there

a grown memorial
whose bone-like roots
can never quench the thirst
of so much weeping,
the memory of stumps
that cares for no confession.

On the long road
the trees do not turn
their faces but upbraid
the wind: *I beseech you
in the bowels of Christ
think it possible
you may be mistaken.*

Reading WSG at Loch Earn

The half-waves of untidal waters wash
a shore of broken ears and bend their glass
to stretch a 'landscape' into something else.

The jetty's rotten teeth are eating air.
The water quickens with its thousand silvery tongues.
Yours is the voice to mend that rock, the thought

that stitch by stitch should quilt itself to nub
the valley's narrow dish. Your unheld
holdings on and back becrannog it.

Here is moss and here is bracken stamped
by thinking tactful of itself. And here is cold,
cold water draining through the stones

yet lapping on in short insistent phrases
that don't end. Above, against, across
the road the burns like tiny murmurs run

from every shrug of moor to fill a loch
which quakes to pass the rumours on to wash
and bless and make the hearing whole,

a speechless doctoring or teasing lip
to thread me through the needle of this place
and tie me here when I am gone.

Trying His Art on Laments

or, trying his art on Laments, he can stand by the cairn of kings,
ken the colour of Fingal's hair, and see the moon-glint on the
hook of the Druids!
—NEIL MUNRO, *The Lost Pibroch*

What the hell happened to the old mechanical Doge?
We thrilled to its promise of a Venice of the Future
but the future is now, and Venice is nowhere to be seen.

What happened to Greek alphabetti spaghetti?
And animate plants? Zero-gravity dice?
And the land between the mountains and the sea?

~

It's true that things are better now,
except for all the things and the definition of 'better'.
We no longer marvel at colour photographs in books;

we no longer have tiny holes drilled into the bones of the face
in order to smuggle vanilla seeds
past the chow chows dozing in every corner of our lives.

We don't any more have to pay rent on our own tongues
or wear phosphorescent hoods
in order to give the sharks time to swim away.

It's true that our nerves are the teeniest bit shot,
but all the pianos and teacups are already smashed
so it hardly matters if our fingers tremble like drunk's.

~

Remember the gas chickens that were only good for soup?
Remember the handwriting prisons and the much-loved skirts of
    wrath?
Your brain cells flee down the chute of promises you made.

Remember the toothache, the old, the bridge and the fair
and the long and the dry and the cool? And the bag
on the back of a cart up a tree in the lane?

Remember the chip pan that bounced on floortiles of cork
and we waited to see who would be splashed
with boiling oil, and who would be spared?

~

This city has built itself around us.
Here's the open sky, and the dawn, and the hod
of stillborn dreams crackling in the hearth.

Here's the usual array of demonic birds.
Here are the eternal stars resolving themselves
into the navigation lights of interstellar freighters

and the rusty bloodstains, the shore and the long rage of the sea,
the curtained windows of buildings that used to be pubs
shimmering behind forcefields of How It Used To Be.

Now the Doge-bot is taking off its cloak
and it's only a dusty old printer. Now the waves
are lapping at the doorsteps of prefabs

we thought had burned down years ago.
Now the floods are rushing inland, and we
are finding it hard to tread water in the canal.

I'd Rather Be in Siena

There will be other meetings,
so let's forgive ourselves
for staring into domes of distance
thinking of our holidays
enjoyed or yet to come.
Your doodles are like the *Maestà* of Duccio.
We are the Nine of the City.
Even the Ecumenical Councils
went like this, in overheated hours
of words well-meant and infinite.

Although our minds are paid for by the company,
our Church and State, we're secretly
daubing at the insides of our skulls
with visions of the land outside the palace,
a vista of acts both unprofessional and free.
The hunters and the goats and lovers
are streaming from the gates
to roam thyme's hillsides and to drink
vin santo, breaking all decrees
with drunken, violent, lustful civility.

What God thinks was agreed
at last by bored old clergymen:
*Each present at the meeting has
two natures . . . one who speaks
and one who dreams . . . So let us dream . . .*
of tidy gardens where the campaniles loom
and higher-ups bring sorbets at our whim

when everything that's said to matter
has been discussed to death and all decisions
for the rest of time are done.

The City to the City

Here engraves itself on every pedestal.
Absorbing all, it takes your word for home
into its grove of archetypes, Piazza of the Names.
Its badge, a sheaf of pillars
held in a loving fist, you hardly notice as you pass
the cardinal bridge of the only river.
Do not protest. You have lingered over
every meal on every terrace.

A clocksmith on a ladder works
to still the hands which radiate
stalled streets of air and plenty.
These houses, row on row, contain
your heart forever. Your head's
the tower cordoned off
hard by the palace walls. Your arm's
a train uncoupled and interred
in the brick and glass duomo of the station.

The only sin is leaving. Think of leaving
and the blue dominions at the end
of yet another lifetime nursing Strega at your table
will reward you with a thousand songs
and all the city's flowers. Leave,
and when they close the gates behind you, you'll forget
each park and window, the very railings
on your favourite boulevard, remembering only
in far burgs of shadows and processions
the wish to settle on a rathaus steps

or low-lipped parapet or by a slim laburnum
and unmarch every aching mile to reach
a *There* which is both origin and grave.

The Abandoned Epic

Where did we leave him? On a peak?
A throne? Declaiming precepts in a waste,
his shining brow disdaining thorny brakes
in frenzied certainty of friendly land
his flair for Being told him we would find?
His gladius was a needle threaded with one thought
which wove a country from the blood of those
who had not luck nor talent to be *these*.
Where's Joan of Arc? Odysseus,
drifting without us on his raft?
Where's Beowulf, feasting in a hall?

Last summer, was it, between books three and four,
I'd had enough of all that gore and certainty
and left the Penguin Classic on a pile
that's now a dusty cliff of layered tales
a bookish archaeologist could sift.
Fanfares wait like tea leaves to unfurl.
No wonder death means nothing to the great
when readers put it off by being bored.

Unread, the mighty metropole declines
though beacons on its walls still burn
as coals the heads of other tribes'
dead champions. Its wars still matter here.
Agnostic priests rush down the corridors of doubt
to find the sanctum locked, and windows barred.
Brooding unconsummated there,
the lantern of the jaw which lights the world's
amazed to hear the world complain

about the shadows that it casts and bring a case
before the international courts.

Gilgamesh must rely on green interpreters.
In anterooms the epics and their virtues wait
to face the judgement of diffuse futurity
and mad with justice, slay the very slain
and torch the ashes of their peoples' funerals.
They wait, in legal transit stripped of rank,
condemned to be an absence from the hearts
who wish the world as simple as its songs.

A Chronicle of the Battle of Poitiers

It was on a flattish landscape of thorns and ditches –
just right for covering yourself in metal
and having a fight in. The French King
had been married at thirteen. The Black Prince
was possessed by the spirit of a glaucous gull.
The Chandos Herald was gouging out on brown
when he wrote this chronicle, giving it
a much dubbier vibe than his later effort, *Agincourt*.
King John said, 'Je m'appelle Jean. J'ai trente-sept ans.'

The French knights rode by in a glittering column.
The Earl of Douglas regretted his life choices.
He had not yet developed
his nervous compulsion for eating string.
When he broke wind, the bad odour
wafted into the noses of Philip the Bold,
the Count of Brienne, Jean de Clermont,
Renaud de Trie, and other flowers of French nobility.
If it seems that there are not many women
in this poem, it should be remembered that
four-fifths of the squires on both sides
were the daughters of rich families
disguised as boys. King John said,
'Y a-t-il une station d'essence à La Rochelle?'

There were the usual hails of arrows,
the usual staggering about,
the usual noble gestures and the usual
exhausted cyborgs of yore stumbling maimed
in a quagmire of hoof prints and dispersed intestines.

The Devil laughed, eating a bag of pears.
A mermaid bathed in a miraculous spring
and many of the men crowded round,
mesmerised by her cod-white breasts,
making it easy for others more chaste
or preferring to lie with boys
to hack off their arms and legs.

Now slaughter really let off the handbrake.
It threw up and went back in for another drink.
Now Gandalf released a storm of flaming hounds,
whose snarls brought many a brawny knecht
to shit his mail. At this point there was no Pope.
Lord Richard of Pembroke grinned: this
was what the fourteenth century was all about.

The French advanced because they thought they should.
Sir John Chandos urged a charge. The Prince said, 'Fuck it,'
and so they did. The King and his son were captured.
It was a major reversal for the French crown.
King John said, 'Est-ce que je peux avoir une bière, s'il vous plaît?'
The Prince hopped around the battlefield,
eating the eyeballs of the slain.

After a Row

I dug a hole to sink these stones our words
among the writhing worm-ends, and unearthed
the bone heap of a burned-down farm,
a pot-bank, half a pair of shears,
a hoard of moss and metal millipedes.
I dug past daytime, past our freshest quarrel
to where the water simmered up and seethed
a warning not to breach the gravel.
Not to be deterred from striking oil,
I shoed my spade again, but when I breached
that veil the black Valhalla showed
a swarm of oozing zombie fossils,
cold superannuated shrimps
haunted for aeons by the thought of fire.
The liquid shadow swallowed my desire.
I sank through slick and lung-refusing stone
and lost the air. Without your breathing close
I choked, exhaled myself, my very voice –
but still I dug, and dug, till I stoved in
the roof of that wide cave which holds the city
which we dreamed of, you and I, the strange mosaic
of semi-precious stones and vatic letters.
I knew then that our whispers could be streets
in that great town that we could never reach.
I fell between the flarings of the city's
domes and spires, down and down
past weathervanes whose pointing was to trouble
and oriel windows where sad children watched
and prayed, in their glass language, for us both.
Below the streets I fell, through grilles and gutters,

sluiced loose-boned down ultra-ancient sewers
where eyeless fishes and the lungless salamander
drowned in the final effluvial sump,
then sank into the silt of lumpy nothing.
At the far end of a long, slow turn I seeped
without ceremony down a tiled drain,
the ultimate rectum of Platonic Down,
and emerged in the vast and violet air to swing,
shivering at the mouth of that pipette
in under-skies more linen-starched than heaven
as in the clouds I thought I heard you smile
until the tension broke, and I went down again.

Outside the Walls

Here is a citadel. Its crystal spires
are lit by braziers of green-flamed fires.
A stone codex that reads itself, its laws
cobble street and lonnen clause by clause.
It is a kitchen where a bullock roasts.
The fat cook grins, repeats the ancient boasts,
takes down a ladle and beclouts the knave
whose bonce is bruised but who is not a slave.
It is a Norman keep, a steepled dome,
a cot to incubate the thought of home.
Five banners fly above its sky to show
the burg is lofty and its burghers know
that boundaries are what define a state,
and on the lintel of the civil gate
an old woman squats, and spreads her parts
to show in entering's where good living starts.
Old aldermen believe in nothing else,
but while they wallow,
                              here, outside the walls
whose carven snarls and arrowslits protect
only those tongues which share a dialect,
a dark figure waits, and can't produce
a valid visa, dodges pots of sluice,
an ex-parishioner, a refugee
whose statelessness condemns him to be free
of all security and walk the lanes
with Fear and Sorrow as his harness chains,
a needimizzler and a dirty tramp
who's undernourished but won't suffer cramp.
Inside his unwalled heart a movement stirs.

His kremlin is a stand of frozen firs
on high ground between that land and this.
His sacred river is a stream of piss.
He takes the remnants of a buzzard's kill,
a sod of grass, a greasy stone, to fill
his children's bellies. Let him take off, and fast,
uncivilly the city's heralds blast
and so he goes, and goes, and beds down in the coombe
to make an Other of the concept Room,
a stanza unconstrained a voice can swell
with told misfortunes to a madrigal.

The Third City

However welcoming the wardens seem,
strange towers which you may not enter loom
in the city of money and the city of love,

and far from either stands a shadowed grove
that smells of camphor and of bergamot.
A passing nomad says, 'Both types of fool

believe one city is the sacred throne,
but neither Caesar nor Jahweh rules so grand
a walled state that they could enclose

the other and digest it whole. They face
uneasily across the plain forever.
To be a citizen is to inhabit both.

You shuttle daily back and forth to weave
a blanket of the double tithes you owe
to warm you in the jackal-haunted night.

There is another place, beyond your sight.
This hidden palace is your yearning's home
where songs and garlands shiver in the air

and every room is open to your hand.'
Then he is no longer standing there
and no third city breaks the desert sands.

Quadrille

Here is a document that says:
A munk of Sinai browt us
Christtis fot. Which means
a mouldy human hock
arrived at Ipswich or
at Boston Stump, and when
it was unwrapped the brethren saw
the biggest toe, old
Father of the Pentateuch,
had been struck off to mutilate
the mutilation, make
a catalectic catalexis of
a verse trod loose from Holy Writ.
And then they saw, in the wrinkled
knuckles of the other four,
a row of Hebrew glyphs to stand
as Tetragrammaton,
divine *love/hate* lined up to name
all shameful shapes, and limp
henceforth as sign, or fake
relic for our missteps' sake.

Þe Scolle on þe Stela

And in Eden I am heer
Saithe þe alabaster Mare
And þe Ratt þat nippes her Heeles
By þe merrie milling Weeles
And þe Catt þat gnaws his Throte
And þe Cankar and þe Stote
And þe Shaddoe in þe Tree
Cast hwere ony Thinge may bee

Heering evry Creaturs call
Except an Angels madrigal
Oneli onn shall paice þe Wall
Wist to go owtwith þe Pale
Hunting for a Manxis Taile
Oneli onn shall Envie shew
Hwat my Bedmate yea and noe
Hwy þe Birddes shold leve me heer
At þe turning of þe Yeare
Hwere þe Doe shall come to Reste
In her alway quickning Breste
Hwy þe broun Tode hwen its dead
Cralls from hwere its buryed
And in Eden hwat is þat
To welcome Maggot Fly and Ratt
To share mie Lofe and in my Bedde
Hwoe shall lissen hwat is sedde
And in Eden hwy do I
Watch mie fafourd Oxen die
See þe Lams þat grase þe Braid
Drownd and dragging in þe Tide

Hwere ys Godde þe onn dimands
Scorning Edens golden Lands
Overwrothe þe Crys to heer
Mounteing up from evry weer

And inn Eden also we
Sunn and Justice and þe Bee
Þe Rockes þe Wrenne and Destinie
As þy Felloes on shall go
Knoweing what þou dost not knowe
Thogh his Name ys in þy Hart
Þou beliefst þy Self apart
Flounceing over Tor and Flod
A thoght unfollowd in þe Woode
Spurneing evry Fruite to finde
Þe Drupe þat ripens in þy Minde
He þe Bayliff strides along
Anxius to destrain þy Song
And choak it in þe Orchards Gloome
Hwile þe Catt and Yaffle croone
Pluck þy Eies and stop þy Eers
To þat Person moving neer
And in Eden I am heer

The Monks' Children

In their religion, monks were allowed to marry,
and indeed several of the monks were women,
and monk was married to monk, and shared a cell,
but the children of such pairs were put to death.
A shame in both senses, their chronicler called it.

Outside the grange a string of oval ponds
was knit by ditch and sluice, fed by the sea.
They laid like venison humbles on the land.
Filled with brine, not bile, these bellies seethed
with a thousand crabs the monks farmed for their meat –
these tiny caparisoned kine crept their cold mead
and ate one another. Thralls ate green nuts.
The monks viewed both species with disdain
but prized the glance of a girl, struck down with fits,
whose mutters they gleaned as a late prophecy.
Their cloisters hummed with hymns of storms and cliffs.
Sea buckthorn graced the carvings on their doors.

The abbot, the best oarsman, issued a decree
careless of custom on his seat of slate
that scythes were not to be leant on the hazel tree;
nor without reason may a person go
beyond the wattle ring to that heaped beach
of the hollow bones of crabs in pinks and creams
and the black of their innards, and other forms,
whose stench brought hungry angels wheeling by.

The Promised Land

It's in the nature of a promised land
that you won't reach it. From the shadeless plains,
oppressed by rulers and their merchant friends,

bereaved by wild dogs and scorpions,
you lurch, whole villages of thwarted wrath,
the sick on mules to give them half a chance,

towards a narrow spur, its tiny grove
where green figs and the water prove your road.
You scale the high couloir, and build stone graves

where children fall or sickness shrinks your load
and by this shaming is your grief annealed:
to lose the weak is tinged with gratitude;

and so you swear, at the edge of a bare wold,
again, to make this journey from a state
of shuttered plenty to an even fold

rich men can scorn and cart their booty out
but may not rule, since you, the people, made
this journey on this date. The way is tight,

and spearmen in the heights leave many dead
as you press through the pass that stretches far
into and through extremities of need;

starvation kills as many and the sores
of grisly plagues confirm that beauty's not
essential to the ways of righteousness.

Our Gods! Our Gods! The convoy quops with fright.
A false Messiah works the troubled line
with rumours of a giant strix that waits

beyond the mountains in your dreams' domain.
Your feet are yielding and the sky is doubt;
six panniers of cheese have lost their brine.

Just then a cry goes up: the furthest scout
has reached the edge of this incessant chain
and seen the way. It is an anguished shout:

what lies below is not the coastal scene
arrayed with vines and creels of winking squid
you had imagined but another plain

as sere and sharpened as the one you fled.
A yellow wolf already teases near.
This land will take some work to make it good;

but even as you gather round to hear
each other's counsel, others turn to go
back through the pass towards the waiting fires

the vengeful rulers there have lit. The you
that was a multitude is now at large
across the slopes of sage and weeping through

this last free night before the homeward march
to servitude and home worse than before:
the evil road, the shame-remembered gulch

and then the plain, where waits the rulers' fire.
From this lone height you watch the darkened gulf
and learn what happens when, as happened here,

a people breaks its promise to itself.

The Lantern

What, then, is the city's source of light?
'Inside the palace on the seventh hill
there is a tomb,' she says, 'not yet in use,

and through its lidless shaft, a kind of well,
they haul, but only God knows how, the rays
that furnaces in other worlds throw out.'

This in the turret of a rounded tower
whose staircase bends against the zodiac
through gardens which reflect the unseen skies.

There is a terrace laid for every sign.
Here is a water garden filled with carp,
and here a ruin where a poison hides,

an archer lounging at a battlement,
a bower where a virgin sleeps, two swards
of herbage fouled on by the goat and ram,

another pool, but here a boy lies drowned,
a pit in which another boy is gored
and then a third, his ribcage eaten out.

Here is a heap of stones where something waits.
Here a mulish court. In this one twins
pursue their selfish incest unconcerned.

'The dagger that you dropped in this strange sky
hoping to leave your crime a jetsam tale
to wash up on a strand where none can parse

its accusation – yet a dogged flare
far off leaks through the toll road of the tomb
towards this tower and its skirts to light

the tussock where, as if it were a bishop's
crozier, the dirtied blade is placed.
You are the Guilty figured in the myth,

so you must leave the city or be killed.'
'But legend says the city walls extend
up to the border of the airless whin

and to the floorless sea, and to the sky
and in the deepest cellar of its crypts
down to the boiling vault of golem's blood

charged by an olden god, deceased, to hold
all men forevermore within its corpse.
Moreover City moves beyond its stone

as model of the mind, as fruit, as name,
unceasingly and by the thought of law.
The city is the language of the world.

Where then, and how, am I to live outwith
the civil caul?' She turns away and stares
across the shadowed vast towards the lamp

formed by the empty tomb upon the hill.
The secret spires and legendary streets
wink their collusion in that stolen glow.

She says that you must enter through the gate
of the seventh palace, break the tomb,
pay off the spirits that are stationed there,

and climb the well towards those other worlds.
'If you arrive beyond the reach of death
then you will be our envoy, and must work

by machinations and by naked force
the immolation of their towns, their church,
their holy wisdoms and their vital arts,

to serve the fire with a foreign love,
with wars nonsensical and vicious too,
a raving to invent a star, to shine

your penance on the city you betrayed
by moving like a constellation through
the troubled heaven of our people's dreams.'

The Graven Pillar

At the city's root
where the future drowns
and water's soaked with stone
there is an empty vault
lit by nightmare fish
that bluely palpitate
around an ancient pillar.
There the rune is carved
that names the girl in search
of whom the sailor came
down from the wincing cliffs
and green imaginings,
the island earldom where
the city is a devil
dreamed in the night.

     (She ran when the hoofs
     drummed by the inn
     the day the stranger's glance
     had quickened at the sheaf
     to turn her gazing from
     the boy of all her life.)

The timid sailor came
and was at once absorbed
by the grinning city,
Stomach-of-the-Clerks.
A mouldy ledger bears
a record of his loss,
unread until the lone
historian of shame,
a starving heretic,

collates such dry remarks
into a shadow song
that conjures and indicts:
> *August Agarttha at*
> *the written canker rots.*
> *A lost girl's cry*
> *unanswered thus infects*
> *the earthen thoroughfares,*
> *the xylem of the Acts*
> *and Instruments at Law*
> *that move a higher world:*
> *it by her murder lacks*
> *its old authority.*

The song itself is stilled,
the scholar put to death
and those who listen pressed
to doubt and let things slide.
The pillar thins. A core
of mineral strength
attenuates both wish
and chains, to leave a guess
in a child's rhyme:
> *The lost seeker must*
> *arrive to find the mark*
> *of the missing corpse.*
> *Then the city falls.*

The Gelding

There was a besom or a hazel broom
which broke when roving janissaries forced
the doorway it was laid across, or housecarls
rather say one source. The splintered end
lay waiting like an asp until the boy
this story dotes on fell to drive a spelk
deep in a heel that later turned the world.
In Kerr's recension he is rendered halt.
Meanwhile the margrave had a creamy colt
it was his wish to geld, to show his power.
He passed the stinking thorp just when the youth
by dint of working with a trenket's spike
had freed the splinter with a wash of blood.
There was a ballad on the subject once.
The margrave blessed him with an office then.
The boy stepped forward and the nervy horse
submitted to the glaive so tenderly
the regal conscience shuddered, and bestowed
the harvest of the country hereabouts,
a shield of or emblazoned with a hand
and promise of a noble girl to wife,
though in the ur-text took the boy himself.
Some figurines portend the wedding fire.
The hero's death upon the flooded plain
years afterwards may be depicted here,
although the crossbow is a late invention.
The boast of him, his fame of luck and virtue
spread in songs and fables like a frith
and when he had enjoyed a hundred slaves
his children scattered down a hundred lanes.

Perhaps this means the progress of the plague.
Some other matter, wrongly copied here.
He laughed and drank, but then began to dream
the cold bewelted torso in the fen
whose bobbing rived the cruck beams of his faith.
The missing cantos made his mission plain.
He told the tale of how he caught the hare
and neither brother then could break the spell
the princeling's hauberk was protected with,
but as the feast went on, the sentries slept.
An incident now hard to grasp occurred.
A robber broke the clasp, and all was lost.
The maiden's crime is not recorded here
but only one wry comment from the scribe:
the second cup was poisoned, not the first.
Escaping by a window, they concealed
themselves in herring barrels, and were drowned.
There is no tale more true to tell than this.

Acknowledgements

Many thanks to the editors of the following publications and projects, for which some of these poems were first produced:

Poetics of the Archive, Butcher's Dog, New Boots and Pantisocracies, Molly Bloom, Antiphon, And Other Poems, The Caught Habits of Language: An Entertainment for W. S. Graham for Him Having Reached One Hundred. 'The Felton Sycamores' was written as part of a collaboration with the composer Cheryl Camm.

I'm deeply grateful to the members of the Northern Poetry Workshop, who have provided me with solidarity, criticism and friendship over the last decade.

This book has been typeset by
SALT PUBLISHING LIMITED
using Sabon, a font designed by Jan Tschichold
for the D. Stempel AG, Linotype and Monotype Foundries.
It is manufactured using Holmen Book Cream 65gsm, a
Forest Stewardship Council™ certified paper from the
Hallsta Paper Mill in Sweden. It was printed and bound
by Clays Limited in Bungay, Suffolk, Great Britain.

CROMER
GREAT BRITAIN
MMXIX